NATIONAL GEOGRAPHIC

The Four Seasons

Simon Lee

Contents

Four Seasons

There are four seasons every year.

Spring

It is spring on the farm.

Which season will be next?

Summer

It is summer on the farm.

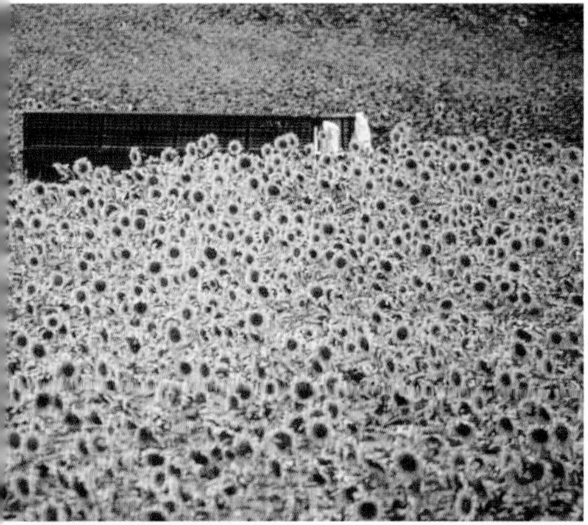

Which season will be next?

Fall

It is fall on the farm.

Which season will be next?

Winter

It is winter on the farm.

Which season will be next?

Spring Again

It is spring again on the farm!